Richmond upon Thames Libraries

Renew online at www.richmond.gov.uk/libraries

First published in Great Britain in 2019
by Wayland

Editor: Victoria Brooker
Produced for Wayland by Dynamo
Written by Pat Jacobs

FSC
www.fsc.org

MIX
Paper from
responsible sources
FSC® C104740

HBK ISBN: 978 1 5263 0970 9
PBK ISBN: 978 1 5263 0971 6

10 9 8 7 6 5 4 3 2 1

Wayland, an imprint of
Hachette Children's Group
Part of Hodder and Stoughton
Carmelite House
50 Victoria Embankment
London EC4Y 0DZ

An Hachette UK Company
www.hachette.co.uk
www.hachettechildrens.co.uk

Printed and bound in China

Picture acknowledgements:

All images courtesy of Gettyimages iStock.

CONTENTS

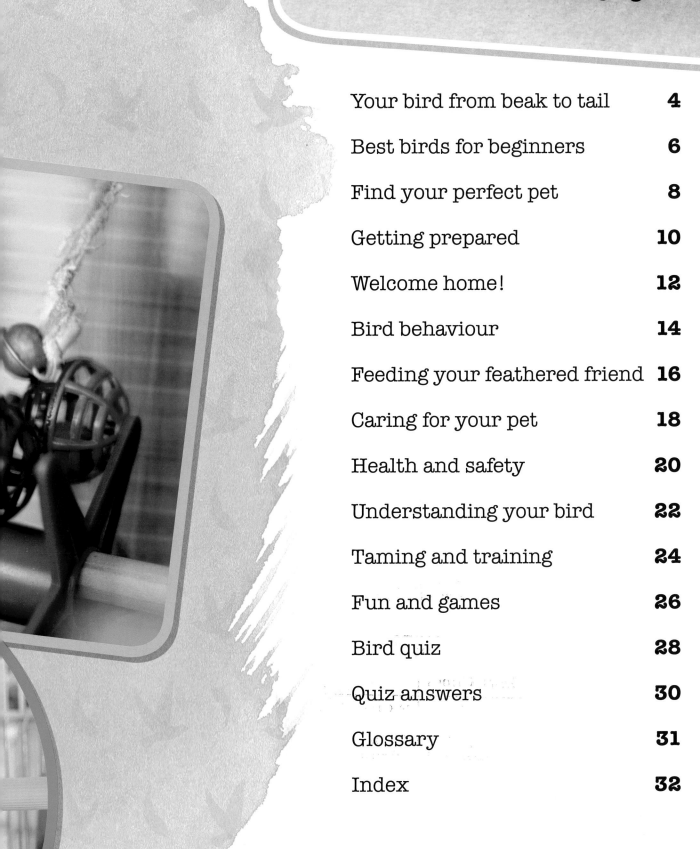

YOUR BIRD
FROM BEAK TO TAIL

Scientists believe birds evolved from small, meat-eating dinosaurs called theropods. Recently found fossils show that some of these creatures from the Cretaceous period had feathers. So, by keeping a pet bird, you're bringing a mini descendant of Velociraptor into your home.

Wings: As wings move down, the flight feathers overlap, push against the air and lift the bird. As they move up, they spread out, letting air pass through.

Cere: This fleshy area above the beak is where the bird's nostrils are located and is the equivalent to our nose.

Ears: Birds have funnel-shaped ears covered with soft feathers.

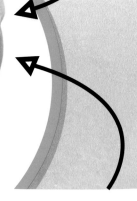

Eyes: Sight is a bird's most important sense. Those with eyes on the sides of their head, can see behind them.

Beak: Birds don't have teeth. They pick up food with their beak and then grind it up in a special part of their stomach, called a gizzard.

Bones: Birds have hollow bones. If they had solid bones, they would be too heavy to fly.

Brain: Although birds have small brains, studies suggest they are clever. In some tests, a parrot did better than a three-year-old child.

Feathers: Birds are the only animals with feathers. They are used for warmth, flight and display. Some are brightly coloured or have a special shape.

Feet: Perching birds have four toes – three facing forwards and one facing back.

BIRD FACTS

- Birds have ultraviolet vision and many birds have markings that reflect UV light, which humans cannot see. For example, male and female blue tits look the same to us, but birds can tell the difference because the feathers on a male's head reflect UV light.

- There are more than 9,000 species of birds and they have colonised all parts of the planet, from the frozen shores of Antarctica to the tropical rainforests.

Tail: Tail feathers are lighter and stiffer than body feathers. Birds use their tails to take off, land and steer during flight. Some fan their tails for display.

BEST BIRDS FOR BEGINNERS

Birds are intelligent and loveable pets but they can be demanding so it's important to choose the right feathered friend for your family. Most birds need hours of attention each day otherwise they get bored and may start destroying furniture and important papers, screeching or feather plucking.

Finches are fast fliers that need plenty of space to exercise. Happiest in small groups twittering to each other all day long, they are great fun to watch.

Budgerigars (or parakeets) are friendly and intelligent. Spend several hours a day with them if you want them to talk. They are happiest in mixed pairs or small groups.

Canaries are perfect if you don't have much space or time. They like to live alone and are bred for their colour, shape and beautiful song. Males are the best songbirds.

Doves are quiet, gentle and easy to tame. They need large cages, with UV lighting if indoors, and plenty of time to fly free. They enjoy being with other doves and their owners.

Parrotlets are little parrots with big personalities and a powerful bite! They are active, loving and demanding, so spend plenty of time with them or they may get aggressive.

Cockatiels are playful pets and you can develop a close bond with them. These intelligent, sociable birds get depressed if left alone, so it's best to get a pair.

Lovebirds are affectionate, inquisitive and sometimes aggressive. It takes patience to tame them and they are noisy birds! One male or a mixed-sex pair make the best pets.

Conures are clever and relaxed. Maroon-bellied, green-cheeked, peach-fronted and dusky-headed conures are the least noisy types.

COCKATOOS AND LARGE PARROTS

Baby cockatoos or macaws can be tempting pets, but these birds live for 60 to 90 years and need a lot of care and space. If unhappy, they may pluck out their feathers, destroy everything in reach, injure people and screech uncontrollably. Many end up in rehoming centres.

FIND YOUR PERFECT PET

When choosing your bird buddy, the first thing to decide is whether you want a beautiful songbird, a calm and gentle companion or an active and playful pet. Do you have lots of spare time to spend with your bird and space for a large cage?

Fancy a chat?

NOISE LEVEL

Canaries, finches or doves may be the best if you or your neighbours don't like noise. Larger parrots screech and shriek, and even budgies and cockatiels can be noisy at times.

TALKING BIRDS

There's no guarantee a bird will talk, but those in the parrot family, such as lovebirds, cockatiels, budgies, parrotlets and conures often do. Males are more likely to talk than females. Some male budgies are real chatterboxes with vocabularies of more than 1,000 words.

BIRDS FOR BUSY PEOPLE

Some birds need lots of company so they don't get bored or depressed. Others can entertain themselves for most of the day, especially when they have toys and cage mates. If you're out most of the day, choose a canary, finches, budgies or doves.

MESSY PETS

All birds throw food about but some are messier than others. Lorikeets need a special diet and so their droppings are especially messy. Cockatiels and doves create a powdery dust when they preen, which can cause allergic reactions.

LIFESPAN GUIDE

Birds are long-lived pets. Here's a guide to their lifespans.

- Canaries and finches: up to 15 years
- Budgerigars: up to 18 years
- Parrotlets and lovebirds: up to 20 years
- Doves: up to 25 years
- Cockatiels: up to 30 years
- Conures: up to 35 years

GETTING PREPARED

Before you collect your new pet, you'll need to have everything ready so they can get settled in right away.

PICK A SPOT

The cage should in a busy part of your home so your pet has plenty of company but not in the kitchen. Fumes from boilers, non-stick pans, cleaning products and gas hobs can be deadly for birds. Your bird will feel safest if its cage is against a wall where it has a good view of the room and won't be startled by everyone's comings and goings. It should be protected from the sun as well as draughts.

EATING AND DRINKING

Food and water hoppers that fit onto the side the cage are a good choice for smaller birds and cut down on mess and waste, but bowls are better for parrots. Those that attach to the side of the cage stop these mischievous birds throwing the bowl around and spilling the food and water. Remember to stock up on food for your pet, too. It's best to stick to the diet your bird is used to at first, and don't forget to get some treats!

UNDERSTAND YOUR PET

We finches like a quieter life than those noisy parrots, so we'll be happy in a room that's less busy, such as a bedroom.

FURNISH YOUR PET'S NEW HOME

Perches give your bird a place to sit and roost. A perch that's the wrong size can harm a bird's feet. Their nails should reach just over halfway around it. Natural wood perches are an essential, while softer rope perches of different sizes will help to exercise your bird's feet.

TOYS

Birds like to keep busy and playing is good exercise when they can't fly about. Toys stop them getting bored and they love to peck and chew, which keeps their beaks in good condition. They will get tired of the same toys so change them frequently.

WELCOME HOME!

Bring your bird home at a quiet time when it can settle in peacefully. Transport your new pet in a secure box with air holes and a towel in the bottom to stop it sliding about. Cover the box with a cloth to make it dark and calming for your bird. Don't put your pet in a car boot because exhaust fumes can be deadly.

SETTLING IN

Put your bird straight into its cage and let it get used to its new home for a couple of weeks before you try to handle it. Meanwhile, chat gently to your pet, quietly change the cage liner and top up the food and water so it can slowly get to know you.

START AS YOU MEAN TO GO ON

Naturally, you'll want to spoil your new feathered friend at first, but birds have good memories. They won't understand if they get less attention and fewer treats after the first few days in their new home. Don't ignore your bird, though. This is the time when you need to build a bond with your new pet.

Make sure perches aren't above food or water dishes. You don't want your pet to foul its food!

BIRD PROOF YOUR HOME

While your bird is settling into its new cage, you can use the time to bird-proof the room, ready for the day you let it out. Birds explore with their beaks and will peck at anything, so now is the time to remove, cover or secure any hazards, including electrical cables, aquariums, breakable objects, household chemicals and other pets!

UNDERSTAND YOUR PET

I'm an escapologist so make sure my cage door has a good lock.

SAFETY FIRST

Never leave a loose bird unattended, especially with a small child or another pet. Birds should not be let out in kitchens or bathrooms – there are too many things there that could harm them. Make sure before you let your bird out that there's no way it could escape (put a note on the door to let other family members know there's a bird on the loose). Turn off ceiling fans and cover windows and mirrors or your bird may try to fly through them.

BIRD BEHAVIOUR

Although your pet's life might be quite different from that of a wild bird, it will still have the same instincts. Understanding how wild birds behave will help you to know if your pet is acting oddly or just being a bird.

PREENING

Feathers are vital to a bird's survival so they spend hours preening them with their beak. As well as removing dust and parasites, preening spreads oil through the feathers and breaks up the downy ones next to the skin to create dust. This oil and dust mix waterproofs the feathers for flying. Sometimes birds preen each other as part of a new relationship ritual. If your bird stops preening, it may be ill or depressed.

BITING

Young birds often peck their owner because they're at the stage where they're exploring everything with their beaks, but as they get older bites can be very painful. Try not to scream because your pet will enjoy your reaction, like biting a squeaky toy. Instead, put the bird down or back in the cage and walk away. Once a bird understands that biting is not rewarded by your attention, it should stop.

FEATHER PLUCKING

Caged birds can pluck out their feathers. Illness or parasites can be a cause so get your pet checked by a vet. Boredom, stress or a poor diet can also be a cause so give your bird attention, change its toys frequently, provide interesting foods and make sure it isn't disturbed by other pets or noise. Loneliness can also be a problem so if they won't stop, get them a companion!

NESTING

In spring, instinct tells birds to find a mate and produce young. Females may lay eggs even if they live alone and males might start collecting nest material. Nesting and sitting on eggs can make birds territorial and aggressive! Reducing your bird's light to less than 12 hours a day by covering the cage may help.

SIGNS OF AFFECTION

Wild birds feed their chicks (and show affection) by bringing up food from their crop and dropping it into the other bird's mouth. Pet birds may bring up food onto their favourite human or toy. Don't be disgusted, it means they love you! Your bird may also preen your hair to show it cares.

TIME FOR BED

A good night's sleep is important for your pet's health. Wild birds go to sleep when it gets dark and wake up at dawn. If your birdcage is in a place where the light is on until late at night, cover it with a cloth or blanket and keep the noise down.

FEEDING YOUR FEATHERED FRIEND

Find out what your new pet has been eating before you bring it home and stick to what it's used to while it settles in. If you want to change your bird's diet, do it slowly, adding new foods a little at a time.

FRESH TREATS

Fruit and vegetables are important for a bird's health. Leafy greens, carrots, peas, broccoli, beans, peppers, corn, fruit and berries are all good additions to your pet's diet, but remove apple and pear pips as they are poisonous to birds. Avoid avocado, onion, rhubarb, mushroom and too much spinach. Clear away leftovers daily.

A BASIC DIET

There are special seed mixtures to make sure each type of pet bird gets all the nutrients it needs. Don't give your bird too much food at once. It will throw it about and pick out the seeds it likes best (usually the most fattening!). Remove all uneaten food at the end of the day.

SET A GOOD EXAMPLE

Just like humans, birds can be suspicious of strange new foods. In the wild, they usually copy what other birds are eating, so if you want your bird to try something new, such as a piece of carrot or a blueberry, let it see you eating it first!

UNDERSTAND YOUR PET

I sometimes enjoy a mashed hard-boiled egg or a few mealworms as a special treat.

Cuttlebone is the internal shell of a cuttlefish. Putting one in your bird's cage is a good way to boost the calcium in its diet. Pecking and biting it provides good exercise for your pet's jaws and helps keep its beak trim.

BIRD GRIT

Wild birds often swallow grit to help them grind up food. The grit goes to a muscly part of their stomach, called the gizzard, where it wears away seed husks so they can digest the seed inside. Most pet birds remove seeds from their husks before eating them, so they don't need grit. Only doves need grit in their diet because they swallow seeds whole.

CARING FOR YOUR PET

It's great to have fun with your bird buddy but keeping a pet comes with responsibilities. These regular tasks will help to keep your feathered friend healthy and safe.

CAGE CLEANING

Dirty cages cause health problems and they smell so keep your cage clean!

Every day
change the floor liner
clean food and water containers
wipe down bars, perches and toys

Every week
wash the floor tray or grate
soak and scrub the perches
clean and change the toys

Every month
scrub, rinse and dry the whole cage

Top Tip! A second, smaller cage makes a safe temporary home for your pet and is useful if it needs to go to the vet.

NAIL TRIMMING

Pet birds need their nails trimming regularly. Before you trim them, find a towel, nail clippers, paper towels, styptic powder and a helper!

- Wrap the bird in the towel, speaking softly and gently to it.

- Ask your helper to gently hold the bird while you clip the sharp, pointed tip of the nail. If you cut too far down, the vein running through the claw will bleed. If this happens, wipe the blood off with a paper towel and dip the wound in styptic powder. Keep an eye on your bird afterwards to make sure the bleeding has stopped.

- Give your bird a treat when you've finished.

WING CLIPPING

Some bird owners clip their pet's wings, while others think it's unnatural and unkind. If done properly, trimming a bird's wing feathers doesn't stop it flying but slows it down. This may mean that your pet gets into less mischief and can be allowed out of its cage more often. Also, clipping may save it from injuring itself in a crowded room. Clipping should never be done before a bird has fully learned to fly. If you decide that wing clipping is right for your bird, ask an expert or a vet to show you what to do – like trimming your nails, it doesn't hurt unless you cut down too far.

PLAYTIME

Allow your bird out of its cage for a few hours each day so it can stretch its wings and explore. The exceptions are canaries and finches. These birds are less easy to tame and you may not be able to get them back into their cage so they need spacious homes.

HEALTH AND SAFETY

Birds are good at hiding signs of illness because they have many predators that would target a weak or sick bird. For this reason it's important to get to know your bird's normal behaviour so you can spot the signs that something is wrong before it's too late.

HOME HAZARDS

Birds are very sensitive to chemicals that are common in our homes. These include the fumes from non-stick pans, insect sprays, bleach, bathroom, oven and window cleaners, body sprays, nail polish, hair dye, scented candles, air fresheners and all forms of smoke. In general, it's best to avoid all sprays and aerosols.

PSITTACOSIS

Psittacosis is a very contagious disease that can be passed to other animals and humans. Symptoms include breathing difficulties, eye infections and loose, watery droppings.

MITES

Mites burrow into a bird's skin and feed on its blood. They are active at night, so watch out for your pet being restless then. Feather damage or crusts on your bird's legs or face are a sign of mites. Check for tiny black or red specks moving on your bird's head and feet at night with a torch and a magnifying glass. Buy anti-mite spray from a vet or pet store.

SIGNS OF ILLNESS

If your bird shows any of these symptoms, you should take it to a vet.

- Sitting at the bottom of the cage with drooping wings, panting and bobbing its tail
- Ruffled feathers that haven't been preened
- Red or runny nose or eyes
- A change in its droppings
- Difficulty breathing
- Weight loss

ULTRAVIOLET LIGHT

Just like humans, birds need ultraviolet light from sunshine to produce vitamin D3. UV light cannot pass through glass so birds that spend all their time indoors are lacking this essential vitamin. Bird experts think that installing a special UV bird lamp could cure many health issues, including feather plucking.

UNDERSTANDING YOUR BIRD

Birds can't always see each other so sound is the best way for them to keep in touch. At close quarters they use body language to get their message across, too.

MAKING A NOISE

Wild birds use their voices to pass on information to others, such as checking in with other members of the flock when they're foraging or travelling, warning that there's a predator nearby and chattering to let other birds know where they are settling down for the night. At dawn, male birds use the power of their songs to show off their health and strength, to attract mates and to defend their territories.

So, if you're looking for a bird that sings or talks, a male is best.

BIRD BODY LANGUAGE

If you understand your bird's actions, you can judge its mood and avoid a painful bite. Here are some common signs to look out for.

- **Freezing**
  A frightened bird may suddenly freeze. This is a defence against predators, who may not notice a motionless bird.

- **Rapid side stepping**
  This means a bird is excited. They often do this when they are pleased to see you!

- **Tail wagging or flipping**
  This is a sign of happiness, like a dog wagging its tail.

- **Eye pinning**
  Parrots can make their pupils larger and

CREST CLUES

When a cockatiel has its crest held back with just the tip tilted up it is happy and relaxed. If the crest is lifted it is excited, and if it is held very high it could mean your bird is scared or over-excited. A flattened crest is a bad sign and means the cockatiel is unhappy or, if it is crouching and hissing, it is feeling aggressive and should be left alone.

UNDERSTAND YOUR PET

I can't reach the top of my head, so if I come towards you with my head bowed and stretched forwards, please scratch me there.

smaller at will. This means they are excited. But if they suddenly fluff up their feathers or fan out their tail, too, they might be angry so stay away!

- **Beak grinding**
  Many birds grind their beaks as they drift off to sleep.

- **Head cocking**
  When a bird cocks its head, it is usually curious and wants to get a better view.

- **Growling or hissing**
  This is a clear warning that the bird wants to be left alone, especially if it's accompanied by eye pinning and raised neck feathers. When this happens, it's best to back off and give your bird buddy some space.

TAMING AND TRAINING

Give your bird at least two weeks to settle in before you start to handle it. Few canaries and finches enjoy being handled but they may step onto your finger if you have a good relationship. The first step is to get your bird used to your hand. Try holding it inside the cage with a treat on the palm and see if your pet will take it. Once your feathered friend associates your hand with a treat, you can teach it to 'step up'.

STEP UP

This is the first command a bird needs to learn. Open the door of the cage and put a treat on your palm, saying the words 'step up' each time you do this. When your bird is used to coming to the door and taking the treat, place your hand in front of the door with the palm facing away from the cage. Hold the treat with your other hand, so your bird has to step onto the side of your index finger to get it. The next stage is to be able to move your hand with your bird standing on it.

STEP DOWN

This is the opposite to 'step up' and you use it when returning your bird to its cage or a perch. Place the hand holding the bird where you want your pet to go. Encourage your pet to step off, saying 'step down'. Give your bird a treat and a good head scratch when it does as you ask so it associates going back to its cage with something pleasant.

IMPORTANT

Every time you open the cage door, there's a chance that your bird might escape, so make sure that the room is bird-proof first.

LEARNING TO TALK

Members of the parrot family, such as budgerigars, parrotlets, lovebirds, conures and cockatiels, can learn to talk but not all will. Some whistle tunes or imitate other noises, such as the phone or the doorbell instead. Male birds are more likely to speak than females. Start by trying to teach your bird a few simple words such as 'hello', 'bye-bye', 'goodnight' and its name. Even if a bird cannot speak, it will often understand what you're saying and obey simple commands.

UNDERSTAND YOUR PET

Sometimes I'm busy doing something else, or just resting, so please leave me in peace if I don't do as you ask.

FUN AND GAMES

Most members of the parrot family are fun-loving creatures and enjoy games such as fetch, peek-a-boo and miniature bird basketball. Keeping them entertained when they're in their cage can be more difficult, so here are a few ideas.

FOODY FUN

Birds have to search for their food in the wild, so make some foraging toys to keep them occupied when they're in their cage. Cut the cardboard tube from a kitchen roll into pieces and hide some treats inside, then fold the ends over. If that's too easy for your pet to undo, tie some string around them (but don't use sticky tape). Thread a selection of washed fruits and vegetables on a string and hang it from the top of the cage for your bird to peck. Include carrot, apple (with the pips removed), broccoli, strawberry, radish, grapes or pepper.

SUPER SHREDDERS

Members of the parrot family love to get their beaks into things and tear them to shreds! Hang some plain cardboard packaging or some new till roll in the cage (it's best to avoid printed paper or card because inks contain chemicals). Make sure there are no staples, tape or patches of glue that could harm your bird, too.

UNDERSTAND YOUR PET

I like toys but if you give me a mirror, I'll think there's another bird in the cage and I won't sing so much.

MAKE A SWING

Make a swing for your bird using a wooden hoop from a craft store. Use a leather lace, rope or a chain to attach it to the top of the cage, and add a bell to the bottom for extra birdy fun.

NATURAL PERCHES

All birds enjoy some natural wood in their cage, either as perches or just to gnaw on, but many common woods are poisonous to pet birds. Here are some that are known to be safe: apple, ash, beech, crab apple, hazel, pear and sycamore. Avoid any trees that may have been sprayed. Remove any moss or lichen, then wash the branches in a bird-safe disinfectant and rinse thoroughly. Bake them in a hot oven for about an hour to kill any bugs or insect eggs and make sure they are cool before you put them in the cage.

HOME TIME

A cage should be a home for your bird, not a prison, so it should be happy to go back there after a few hours of freedom. Make sure your pet is hungry, then before it goes back put some of its favourite food in the cage. It's useful to have a signal to tempt it back, too, such as tapping the cage or ringing a bell.

BIRD QUIZ

How much do you know about your feathered pal? Take this quiz to find out.

1 **What is a bird's cere?**

a. The area above its beak that includes its nostrils

b. An organ that grinds up food

c. A part of the tail

2 **Which birds like to live alone?**

a. Doves

b. Budgerigars

c. Canaries

3 **Which birds are most likely to talk?**

a. Females

b. Males

c. No difference

4 Which of these birds lives longest?

a. Finches
b. Conures
c. Doves

5 Which of these foods is not suitable for birds?

a. Avocado
b. Rhubarb
c. Both of these

6 What is a good source of calcium for your bird?

a. Cuttlefish bone
b. Carrot
c. Mushroom

7 How often should you change the floor liner in your pet's cage?

a. Every week
b. Every day
c. Every month

8 What could be the cause if your bird is suddenly restless at night?

a. It may have mites
b. It is bored
c. The room is too noisy

9 What does it mean when a bird is 'eye pinning'?

a. Staring at its reflection in a mirror
b. Looking its owner straight in the eye
c. Making the pupils of the eye larger and smaller

10 What does it mean if a bird steps quickly from side to side?

a. It is frightened
b. It is excited
c. Its feet are painful

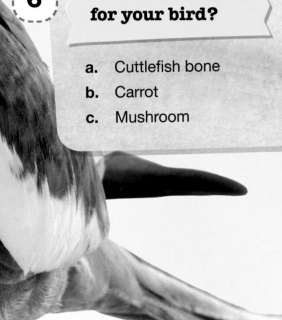

QUIZ ANSWERS

1 What is a bird's cere?

a. The area above its beak where its nostrils are located

2 Which birds like to live alone?

c. Canaries

3 Which birds are most likely to talk?

b. Males

4 Which of these birds lives longest?

b. Conures

5 Which of these foods is not suitable for birds?

c. Both of these

6 What is a good source of calcium for your bird?

a. Cuttlefish bone

7 How often should you change the floor liner in your pet's cage?

b. Every day

8 What could be the cause if your bird is suddenly restless at night?

a. It may have mites

9 What does it mean when a bird is 'eye pinning'?

c. Making the pupils of the eye larger and smaller

10 What does it mean if a bird steps quickly from side to side?

b. It is excited

GLOSSARY

aggressive – Likely to attack.

colonise – To go and live in an area.

contagious disease – An illness that is easily spread from one animal to another.

crest – A tuft of feathers on a bird's head, which is used for display and communication.

Cretaceous – The period from 145 to 66 million years ago, when most dinosaurs were alive.

crop – A pouch in a bird's throat where food is stored.

cyanide – A deadly poison. Some fruit seeds, such as apple, contain a substance that can produce cyanide in the body if they are chewed and swallowed.

descendant – A relation of a person or animal that lived in the past.

downy – Soft, fluffy feathers that keep a bird warm.

evolve – To develop slowly or change over generations.

foraging – To search for food.

gizzard – A part of the stomach with thick, muscly walls where birds store grit to grind up hard foods.

hopper – A container with an opening at the bottom, which can be fixed to a cage so that food or water drop down into a small bowl.

imitate – To copy.

mite – A tiny bug related to a spider. Bird mites feed on a bird's blood and cause itching.

mixed-sex pair – A male and a female bird.

nutrients – The substances in food, such as protein and vitamins that help animals to grow and keep them healthy.

parasite – An animal that lives in or on another creature and feeds from it (often by sucking its blood).

predator – An animal that hunts and eats other creatures.

preen gland – An organ that produces oil for water–proofing a bird's feathers

preen – To clean and straighten feathers.

pupil – The black part of the eye.

roost – settle down to sleep.

styptic powder – A powder that stops bleeding by sealing the injured vein.

territorial – The way a bird behaves when it is defending its nesting site.

theropod – A small meat-eating dinosaur that ran on its hind legs.

ultraviolet (UV) light – The light that makes up about 10% of sunlight and is divided into UVA, UVB and UVC. Humans cannot see UV light but birds can. Some have patterned feathers that reflect UVA light and help them to recognise each other. UVB light produces vitamin D3 in the body, which is important for good health. Most UVC rays do not reach Earth.

Velociraptor – A small meat-eating dinosaur that had feathers.

INDEX